Tiny Talks

Volume 7
I'll Follow Him in Faith

A year's worth of simple messages that can be given during Primary or Family Home Evening

Other children's books by Lee Ann Setzer

I Am Ready for Baptism
A fun activity book for children preparing for baptism.

Sariah McDuff: Primary Program Diva
The annual Primary program in sacrament meeting seems like the perfect place for Sariah to try out her new superstar rock singer act!

Sariah McDuff: Christmas Detective
What do you get for the girl who doesn't want anything that most kids want? Sariah, her offbeat family, and her funny Primary class find the true spirit of Christmas.

Sariah McDuff: Valentine's Day Scrooge
What is the true meaning of Valentine's Day if you're seven years old and you hate boys?

Sariah McDuff Will Walk with You
The Primary president wants Sariah to make friends with a girl who's very different.

**Volume 7
I'll Follow Him in Faith**

A year's worth of simple messages
that can be given during Primary
or Family Home Evening

by Lee Ann Setzer
Illustrated by Glenn Harmon

**CFI
Springville, Utah**

© 2006 Lee Ann Setzer

All rights reserved.

This book is not an official publication of The Church of Jesus Christ of Latter-day Saints.

No part of this book may be reproduced in any form whatsoever, whether by graphic, visual, electronic, film, microfilm, tape recording, or any other means, without prior written permission of the author, except in the case of brief passages embodied in critical reviews and articles.

ISBN: 1-55517-922-3
e.1

Published by CFI,
an imprint of Cedar Fort, Inc.
925 N. Main, Springville, Utah, 84663
www.cedarfort.com

Distributed by:

Cover design © 2006 by Lyle Mortimer
Illustrations © 2006 by Glenn Harmon

Printed in the United States of America
10 9 8 7 6 5 4 3 2 1

Printed on acid-free paper

To Jack, who helped

Table of Contents

Introduction — viii

Chapter 1: January: I Have Faith in the Lord Jesus Christ — 1

Chapter 2: February: My faith in Jesus Christ grows when I know who He is — 7

Chapter 3: March: My faith in Jesus Christ grows when I follow His example and keep His commandments — 13

Chapter 4: April: My faith in Jesus Christ grows when I know He is my Savior and Redeemer — 19

Chapter 5: May: My faith in Jesus Christ grows when I learn about the restoration of the gospel — 25

Chapter	6:	June: I follow Jesus Christ in faith when I make and keep my baptismal covenants	31
Chapter	7:	July: My family can follow Jesus Christ in faith	37
Chapter	8:	August: My faith in Jesus Christ grows when I listen to the Holy Ghost	43
Chapter	9:	September: My faith in Jesus Christ grows when I serve others	49
Chapter	10:	October: I show my faith in Jesus Christ when I share the gospel with others	55
Chapter	11:	November: My faith in Jesus Christ blesses my life. I am thankful for my blessings	61
Chapter	12:	December: Jesus Christ once lived on the earth, and I have faith that He will come again	67

Introduction

Welcome to the seventh volume of the *Tiny Talks* series! This book follows the 2007 Primary theme, "I'll Follow Him in Faith." This year's theme focuses on building faith in the Lord Jesus Christ.

These tiny talks are for children, parents, families, and Primaries. They can, of course, provide emergency relief when everyone remembers at the last minute that someone has a talk to give in Primary! Each talk includes a scripture, and most include a suggested visual aid from the Gospel Art Picture Kit (GAPK), including the supplement pack. Occasionally, the visual is a readily available item such as a copy of the *Ensign* or the fingers on your hand.

Of course, the ideal for talks in Primary is that children will prepare beforehand, using their own insights and stories and their own words. This year the talks include Thought Questions, which encourage children to remember their own experiences, bear their testimonies, and put themselves in the position of the characters in the stories.

You might use these tiny talks as starting points for discussions in family home evening or as references for sharing time presentations and the children's sacrament meeting presentation. I hope that children will enjoy reading and talking about this book on their own. I hope you enjoy this little book!

Chapter 1

January: I Have Faith in the Lord Jesus Christ

*If ye have faith ye hope for things
which are not seen, which are true.*

—Alma 32:21

Scripture:
And now as I said concerning faith—faith is not to have a perfect knowledge of things; therefore if ye have faith ye hope for things which are not seen, which are true (Alma 32:21).

Visual Aid:
GAPK 617
Search the Scriptures

1. I have faith in the Lord Jesus Christ. Faith means trust.

The prophet Alma once met some people who wanted to worship God. They asked him what they should do. Alma told them that faith is like a seed that we plant in our hearts. The seed can even be a desire to believe, or a "particle" of faith. If it is a good seed, it will grow. When the seed of faith grows inside us, it brings good feelings. We feel peace, light, and understanding. We can take good care of the seed so that it will grow. We can pray, study the scriptures, and keep the commandments. This helps the seed of faith grow. Someday, Alma says, our seed of faith will become a "tree" of eternal life (Alma 32:27, 37–41).

Thought Question: How have you helped your seed of faith grow?

2. Faith in the Lord Jesus Christ is the first principle of the gospel.

Jesus was walking one day when a blind man called out to him. Jesus stopped, asked the blind man to come to Him, and asked what he wanted. The blind man begged Jesus to heal his eyes. Jesus said, "Thy faith hath made thee whole." Suddenly, the man could see! He joyfully followed Jesus.

Faith is the first principle of the gospel. Jesus asks all of us to come unto Him. We trust that Jesus can help us, heal us, and guide us. When we reach out to Him, we always find that He is waiting for us. He can forgive us, make us pure, give us help and comfort, and lead us home to Him. But first we have to believe.

Thought Question: How has your faith in Jesus Christ blessed you?

Scripture:
And Jesus said unto him, Go thy way; thy faith hath made thee whole. And immediately he received his sight, and followed Jesus in the way (Mark 10:46).

Visual Aid:
GAPK 213
Christ Healing a Blind Man

3. My faith in Jesus Christ is strengthened when I pray.

Scripture

And it came to pass that after I had prayed and labored with all diligence, the Lord said unto me: I will grant unto thee according to thy desires, because of thy faith (Enos 1:12).

The prophet Enos in the Book of Mormon went hunting in the wilderness. He thought about his sins. He thought about all the things his father had taught him about Jesus. Enos started to pray for forgiveness. He prayed for hours and hours. His prayer was hard work. Enos said he "wrestled," "struggled," "labored," "hungered," and "cried" in his prayer. At last, Heavenly Father answered the prayer of Enos. He forgave Enos. Because of his faith and prayer, Enos felt Heavenly Father's love (Enos 1:2, 4, 10, 12, 15).

Sometimes we have to work hard like Enos when we pray. But if we pray in faith, Heavenly Father will always answer. His answer will strengthen our faith.

Thought Questions: How have your prayers been answered? How could you improve your prayers?

Visual Aid:
GAPK 305
Enos Praying

4. I have faith in the Lord Jesus Christ. He will help me keep the commandments.

Joseph Smith was fourteen years old when Heavenly Father made him a prophet. When Joseph Smith was twenty-one, Heavenly Father commanded him to translate the golden plates. The golden plates were written in a language that no one understood. Joseph could not translate them by himself. No one could. Joseph was very young. He only had about a third-grade education. How could such a boy do something so difficult and important?

Joseph believed in Heavenly Father. He had faith that God would help him. Joseph Smith translated hundreds of pages in only eighty-five days.

If Heavenly Father commands us to do something, He will help us do it. We may have to work hard. We may not get it right the first time. But He will not let us fail. Our faith will grow when we see His help.

Thought Question: How has Heavenly Father helped you keep His commandments?

Scripture
And it came to pass that I, Nephi, said unto my father: I will go and do the things which the Lord hath commanded, for I know that the Lord giveth no commandments unto the children of men, save he shall prepare a way for them that they may accomplish the thing which he commandeth them (1 Nephi 3:7).

Visual Aid:
GAPK 416
Translating the Book of Mormon

Chapter 2

February: My faith in Jesus Christ grows when I know who He is

And we believe and are sure that thou art that Christ, the Son of the living God.

—John 6:69

1. Jesus Christ is Heavenly Father's firstborn Son. I also am a child of God.

Scripture

And he said unto them, How is it that ye sought me? wist ye not that I must be about my Father's business? (Luke 2:49)

When Jesus was a boy, His family went to Jerusalem every spring for the Passover. The year He was twelve, they all went as usual. On the way home, His mother realized that Jesus was missing! Mary and Joseph hurried back to Jerusalem. They looked and looked for Jesus. Finally they found Him in the temple. The wise and educated teachers were listening to Him teach and were asking Him questions. The teachers couldn't believe how wise the young boy Jesus was. Mary asked Jesus why He had stayed behind. Jesus told her that He needed to do His "Father's business" (Luke 2:42–51).

Even as a young boy, Jesus knew that He was God's Son. He knew He had a special mission.

We are all children of God. He gave each one of us a special mission. Like Jesus, we need to remember who we are. We do this by seeking His help and by serving His children.

Thought Question: How does knowing you are a child of God help you at school, at home, or with your friends?

Visual Aid:
GAPK 205
Boy Jesus in the Temple

2. Heavenly Father has a plan for me. Jesus Christ and His Atonement are central to this plan.

The Lord called Enoch to be a prophet. He promised to help Enoch. He told Enoch, "Walk with me" (Moses 6:34).

The Savior Jesus Christ is very important to the plan of salvation. In the pre-earth life, Heavenly Father asked for someone to be our Savior. Jesus loved us. He agreed to suffer and die for us. He also created the earth for us.

In this life, we cannot remember our pre-earth life. We can make our own choices. We have to have faith in Heavenly Father's plan. The Savior's Atonement allows us to repent when we sin. The Savior sends His Spirit to help us.

Someday everyone will be resurrected because of Jesus' Atonement. If we have accepted His gospel, His Atonement will save us from our sins. If we walk with Him and keep His commandments, we can live with Jesus, Heavenly Father, and our families forever.

Thought Question: What can you do to follow Heavenly Father's plan for you?

Scripture
Behold my Spirit is upon you, wherefore all thy words will I justify; and the mountains shall flee before you, and the rivers shall turn from their course; and thou shalt abide in me, and I in you; therefore walk with me (Moses 6:34).

Visual Aid:
GAPK 239
The Resurrected Jesus Christ

Scripture

And behold, all things have their likeness, and all things are created and made to bear record of me, both things which are temporal, and things which are spiritual; things which are in the heavens above, and things which are on the earth, and things which are in the earth, and things which are under the earth, both above and beneath: all things bear record of me (Moses 6:63).

Visual Aid:
GAPK 600
The World

3. Jesus Christ created the earth as a place for us to live and gain experience.

In the Book of Mormon, an evil man named Korihor started teaching that no Savior would come. Korihor said he would believe in God if he saw a sign. The prophet Alma told him that "all things" show that God lives (Alma 30:44). When we see the earth, the sky, and the sun, moon, and stars, we can know that God created them (Moses 6:63). We can know that He made the earth for us.

Heavenly Father made the earth for a reason. He sent us here to learn faith in Jesus Christ and to choose the right. Then we can return to live with our Heavenly Father someday.

Thought Question: Which of God's creations are your favorites?

4. Jesus Christ lived on earth. His teachings and miracles blessed the lives of the people.

Jairus was a leader of the Jewish people in Jesus' time. One day his daughter became very ill. Jairus asked Jesus to come and heal her. On the way, Jesus stopped to heal and bless someone. Jairus's friends came and said the girl had already died, so Jesus shouldn't bother to come. Jesus said, "Be not afraid, only believe. . . . [She] is not dead, but sleepeth." The people all laughed at Him. When He reached the house, He made everyone except the girl's parents and three of His disciples leave. Then He took the girl by the hand and told her to "arise." The girl stood up and walked. The people were surprised. Jesus had healed Jairus's daughter by the power of God (Mark 5:36, 39, 41).

Thought Question: How has Jesus blessed your life?

Scripture
As soon as Jesus heard the word that was spoken, he saith unto the ruler of the synagogue, Be not afraid, only believe (Mark 5:36).

Visual Aid:
GAPK 215
Jesus Blessing Jairus's Daughter

Chapter 3

March: My faith in Jesus Christ grows when I follow His example and keep His commandments

Follow me, and do the things which ye have seen me do.

—2 Nephi 31:12

1. Jesus Christ's life is an example to me.

After the Savior was resurrected, He visited the people in America. He let them come to Him, one by one. He showed them the nail marks in His hands. He let them touch the sword wound in His side. Each one of them knew He was the Savior because they all felt and saw Him.

Finally everyone had seen, touched, and met the Savior. He told them that they should follow His example. They should not tell anyone to go away. Everyone should get a chance to "feel and see" (3 Nephi 18:25).

Of course, we can't show the Savior to our friends. But we can invite them to church so they can feel the Spirit. We can help them see the power of God in our lives and theirs. Then we will be following Jesus' example.

Thought Question: How can you help others "feel and see" the Savior's love?

Scripture
And ye see that I have commanded that none of you should go away, but rather have commanded that ye should come unto me, that ye might feel and see; even so shall ye do unto the world
(3 Nephi 18:25).

Visual Aid:
GAPK 316
Jesus Teaching in the Western Hemisphere

2. I will study the scriptures and pray.

When he was a boy, Joseph Smith lived in a place with many different churches. Everyone was excited about choosing a church to join. Joseph Smith attended meetings at the churches, but he did not know which church was right and true.

One night he read James, chapter 1, verse 5, in the Bible. It said that anyone who "lack[s] wisdom" should "ask of God," and God would answer. Joseph thought and thought about this scripture. He knew that he needed wisdom from God. Finally, he decided to pray.

When Joseph prayed, Heavenly Father and Jesus Christ appeared to him. They told him not to join any of the churches. They told him he was to become a prophet (Joseph Smith–History, 1:1–26).

Like the Prophet, we can read the scriptures and pray. Heavenly Father will teach us and help us through the scriptures.

Thought Question: How has Heavenly Father taught you through the scriptures?

Scripture
If any of you lack wisdom, let him ask of God, that giveth to all men liberally, and upbraideth not; and it shall be given him (James 1:5).

Visual Aid:
GAPK 402
Joseph Smith Seeks Wisdom in the Bible

3. I will keep the Sabbath day holy.

Scripture
And he said unto them, The sabbath was made for man, and not man for the Sabbath (Mark 2:27).

One Sabbath day, Jesus and His followers were walking by a field of corn. His followers picked a few ears of corn to eat. Leaders who feared Jesus said that no one should pick corn on the Sabbath. They wanted the people to stop following Jesus.

Jesus replied, "The sabbath was made for man, and not man for the sabbath" (Mark 2:27).

The Sabbath day is a gift that Heavenly Father made for us. When we keep the Sabbath day holy, we grow closer to our Savior. We can feel His Spirit more strongly. We get ready to face a new week with his help.

Thought Question: How has keeping the Sabbath blessed your life?

Visual Aid:
GAPK 237
Jesus at the Door

4. I will keep the commandments and live now to be worthy to go to the temple.

Jesus told a story about ten young women getting ready for a wedding at night. They had oil lamps. Five of the young women had plenty of oil. Their lamps were ready when the wedding started. Five did not have enough oil. Their lamps went out. They were not ready when the wedding started (Matthew 25:1–9).

The oil in this story reminds us of the things we need to do to prepare for the future. President Spencer W. Kimball said we get this oil "drop by drop."[1] We get it by keeping the commandments, praying, repenting, and serving others. We make important decisions every day. Should I lie if no one will find out? Should I break the Word of Wisdom so people will be friends with me? We will be ready to choose the right if we have prepared. And we will be able to have the blessings of the temple if we have made good choices.

Thought Question: How are you preparing to make good choices, one small step at a time?

Scripture
For behold, this life is the time for men to prepare to meet God; yea, behold the day of this life is the day for men to perform their labors (Alma 34:32).

Visual Aid:
GAPK 502
Salt Lake Temple

Chapter 4

April: My faith in Jesus Christ grows when I know He is my Savior and Redeemer

For God so loved the world, that he gave his only begotten Son, that whosoever believeth in him should not perish, but have everlasting life.

—John 3:16

Scripture
And behold, I am the light and the life of the world; and I have drunk out of that bitter cup which the Father hath given me, and have glorified the Father in taking upon me the sins of the world, in the which I have suffered the will of the Father in all things from the beginning (3 Nephi 11:11).

Visual Aid:
GAPK 240
Jesus the Christ

1. Jesus Christ is my Savior and Redeemer. He came into the world to do the will of the Father.

In the pre-earth life, we "shouted for joy" when we heard about Heavenly Father's plan of salvation (Job 38:7). More than anything, we wanted to grow to be like Him.

But no one besides Heavenly Father and Jesus is perfect. Everyone who knows good from evil makes wrong choices sometimes. We needed someone to save us from our sins. That person would have to suffer for our sins. Jesus loved us. He said He would go down to earth and be our Savior. He kept His promise to us.

We can rely on Jesus. Elder Jeffrey R. Holland said that after all Jesus has been through for us, "He is not going to turn His back on us now."[2]

Thought Question: How do you feel when you think about Jesus' love for us?

2. Because of the Atonement and Resurrection of Jesus Christ, I will be resurrected.

President Heber J. Grant lost many family members to death. His little boy, Heber Stringham Grant, was sick for more than a year. President Grant spent hours by young Heber's bed, trying to help and comfort him. He spent as much time in his son's room as he could. When little Heber died, President Grant was very sad. But he also felt "a peaceful influence, a comfort, and a joy." He knew that someday his little son would be resurrected. He knew he would see him, hold him, talk with him, and play with him again.[3]

Everyone will be resurrected with a perfect body that can never die again. Resurrection is a great gift from our Savior, Jesus Christ.

Thought Question: How has knowing about the Resurrection comforted or blessed you?

Scripture
For as in Adam all die, even so in Christ shall all be made alive
(1 Corinthians 15:22).

Visual Aid:
GAPK 512
Heber J. Grant

3. Because of the Atonement, I can repent and return to live with Heavenly Father and Jesus Christ.

Scripture

But remember, God is merciful; therefore, repent of that which thou hast done which is contrary to the commandment which I gave you, and thou art still chosen, and art again called to the work (D&C 3:10).

Many friends helped the Prophet Joseph Smith while he was translating the Book of Mormon. One friend, Martin Harris, kept asking the Prophet to let him show the translation to some friends. The Prophet asked Heavenly Father. Heavenly Father replied again and again that Joseph must not let Martin take the translation.

At last, when Joseph asked again, Heavenly Father told him to go ahead and let Martin have 116 pages of the Book of Mormon. Martin took the pages, but he lost them. The Lord told the Prophet not to translate them again.

The Prophet felt terrible for losing the pages. He was not allowed to translate for a while. But the Prophet repented. His gift and his calling returned to him. He continued in faith until the end of his life (D&C 3).

Even the Prophet Joseph Smith needed repentance. We also need it—every day. Through Jesus Christ's love, we can become clean again.

Thought Question: How has repentance blessed your life?

Visual Aid:
GAPK 401
The Prophet Joseph Smith

4. My faith in Jesus Christ grows when I hear the apostles and prophets testify of Him.

Our lives here on earth are a test. We have to walk by faith. That means that we had to forget our pre-earth life. We can't remember living as spirits with our Heavenly Father. We can't remember the promises we made to Him or that He made to us. We can't see His face or hear His voice for now.

But Heavenly Father has given us a way to hear His voice. He says that listening to the prophets and apostles is "the same" as listening to His own voice. The prophets can lead us back to Heavenly Father if we listen to them and obey their words (D&C 1:38).

Thought Question: How do you feel when you listen to the prophet's testimony?

Scripture
What I the Lord have spoken, I have spoken, and I excuse not myself; and though the heavens and the earth pass away, my word shall not pass away, but shall all be fulfilled, whether by mine own voice or by the voice of my servants, it is the same (D&C 1:38).

Visual Aid:
Center page showing general authorities in the latest general conference issue of the *Ensign*

Chapter 5

May: My faith in Jesus Christ grows when I learn about the restoration of the gospel

*Therefore, behold, I will proceed to do
a marvellous work among this people, even
a marvellous work and a wonder.*

—Isaiah 29:14

Scripture
And he shall send Jesus Christ, which before was preached unto you: Whom the heaven must receive until the times of restitution of all things, which God hath spoken by the mouth of all his holy prophets since the world began (Acts 3:20–21).

Visual Aid:
GAPK 509
Wilford Woodruff

1. The Lord restored the fulness of the gospel through Joseph Smith.

After Jesus had returned to Heavenly Father and His apostles had died, people started changing His true Church. Heavenly Father took away the priesthood. There were no more prophets. Many wise and good people searched the scriptures and prayed for God to restore His true Church.

When President Wilford Woodruff was a young man, he wished to find the true Church. He knew this church would have revelation, miracles, and the priesthood of God. He said, "I prayed night and day that I might see a prophet. I would have gone a thousand miles to have seen a prophet." At last he met missionaries from The Church of Jesus Christ of Latter-day Saints. They taught him that God had restored the truth through Joseph Smith. Wilford Woodruff was baptized. He spent the rest of his life teaching that Jesus Christ's Church was restored.[4]

Thought Question: What blessings have come to you because of the restoration of the gospel?

2. Joseph Smith translated the Book of Mormon through the power of God.

It took the Prophet Joseph Smith about three months to translate the Book of Mormon. One day, when the Prophet was going to work on the translation, he and his wife had a disagreement. After the disagreement, the Prophet tried to translate, but he couldn't do it. Not one word would come.

The Prophet went to the woods and prayed for forgiveness. He found Emma and apologized for arguing with her. Then he went back to work translating. Now that his bad feelings were gone, he could translate. The Prophet could only translate the Book of Mormon when he had the Spirit of God. The Book of Mormon came to us from God, through the Prophet Joseph Smith.[5]

Thought Question: What verses in the Book of Mormon have helped you or touched your heart?

Scripture
Behold, here is wisdom; yea, to be a seer, a revelator, a translator, and a prophet, having all the gifts of God which he bestows upon the head of the church (D&C 107:92).

Visual Aid:
GAPK 401
The Prophet Joseph Smith

3. The Book of Mormon is the word of God and is another testament of Jesus Christ.

Scripture
Proving to the world that the holy scriptures are true, and that God does inspire men and call them to his holy work in this age and generation, as well as in generations of old (D&C 20:11).

The prophet Jacob in the Book of Mormon once met an evil man named Sherem. Sherem taught that Jesus Christ would never come. Jacob asked Sherem if he believed the scriptures. Sherem said he did. Jacob replied that if he understood the scriptures, he would believe in the Savior. He said that every prophet had taught about Jesus Christ (Jacob 7:11).

Every page of the Book of Mormon—even the front cover—testifies of Jesus Christ. The Book of Mormon tells of the time that Jesus visited His people in the Americas. It teaches about the Savior's Atonement. It helps explain many things in the Bible. The Bible and the Book of Mormon work together to teach us about our Savior.

Thought Question: Can you bear your testimony of the Book of Mormon?

Visual Aid:
GAPK 326
The Bible and Book of Mormon: Two Witnesses

4. The priesthood was restored. A living prophet leads the Church under the direction of Jesus Christ.

Oliver Cowdery helped Joseph Smith translate the Book of Mormon. He wrote down what the Prophet said as he translated. One day the Prophet was translating a story about baptism for the remission of sins. To learn more about baptism, Joseph and Oliver went to the woods to pray. John the Baptist appeared to them. He gave them the Aaronic Priesthood and told them to baptize each other. He also promised them that soon they would receive the Melchizedek Priesthood. Oliver and Joseph were filled with joy (Joseph Smith–History 1:66–73).

The priesthood is the power and authority to act in the name of God. People can say they have power and authority, but only Heavenly Father can give men the true priesthood. It had to come to the Prophet from Heavenly Father.

Thought Question: How has the priesthood blessed your life?

Scripture
We believe that a man must be called of God, by prophecy, and by the laying on of hands by those who are in authority, to preach the Gospel and administer in the ordinances thereof (Articles of Faith 1:5).

Visual Aid:
GAPK 407
John the Baptist Conferring the Aaronic Priesthood

Chapter 6

June: I follow Jesus Christ in faith when I make and keep my baptismal covenants

I say unto thee, Except a man be born of water and of the Spirit, he cannot enter into the kingdom of God.

—John 3:5

1. Jesus Christ was baptized.

Scripture
But John forbad him, saying, I have need to be baptized of thee, and comest thou to me? And Jesus answering said unto him, Suffer it to be so now: for thus it becometh us to fulfil all righteousness. Then he suffered him (Matthew 3:14–15).

John the Baptist was a prophet at the Savior's time. He went out in the desert and preached to the people. He taught them about baptism. He taught them that the Savior would soon come.

At last the Savior came out to the desert. He asked John to baptize Him. John said no. John said he wasn't good enough to baptize the Savior. But Jesus told him that he must do it "to fulfil all righteousness" (Matthew 3:15). That meant that even though Jesus had no sins to wash away, He still needed to be baptized. Everyone must be baptized to be part of Jesus Christ's true Church, so John baptized Jesus.

When Jesus came out of the water, the Holy Ghost came down upon Him in the form of a dove. His work on the earth had begun.

Thought Question: How do you feel about your own baptism?

Visual Aid:
GAPK 208
John the Baptist Baptizing Jesus

2. When I am baptized, I make sacred covenants with Heavenly Father.

When President Howard W. Hunter was a young boy, he saw some big boys throw a tiny kitten in the water. He waited until the boys had left, and then he pulled the kitten out. Praying all the way home, he brought it to his mother.

Sister Hunter's eyes filled with tears when she saw the kitten. She told Howard that the kitten might not live. But she promised to try to help it. She wrapped the kitten in a quilt and put it in a warm place in the kitchen. Howard worried all night. But in the morning, he heard the kitten meowing. He ran to the kitchen. The kitten was walking around and crying for milk. He knew the kitten would be all right.[6]

When we are baptized, we promise to help others. President Hunter's kindness saved the kitten's life. He kept his baptism promise.

Thought Question: What are some ways we can keep our baptismal covenants?

Scripture
Now I say unto you, if this be the desire of your hearts, what have you against being baptized in the name of the Lord, as a witness before him that ye have entered into a covenant with him, that ye will serve him and keep his commandments, that he may pour out his Spirit more abundantly upon you? (Mosiah 18:10)

Visual Aid:
GAPK 519
Howard W. Hunter

3. After I am baptized, I will be confirmed and receive the Holy Ghost.

Once you've been baptized, you are ready to receive an important and wonderful gift from our Heavenly Father. Priesthood holders will lay their hands on your head and command you to receive the Holy Ghost. They will also confirm you a member of The Church of Jesus Christ of Latter-day Saints.

Elder Richard G. Hinckley has invited everyone in the Church to get a little notebook and start a list with the title "What my membership in The Church of Jesus Christ of Latter-day Saints means to me." He says that your list will fill you with gratitude for your membership.[7] Your list could include your testimony, guidance from the Holy Ghost, good friends who share your values, and teachers and leaders who care about you. Membership in the Church is a great blessing.

Thought Question: What blessings have you received from belonging to the Church?

Scripture
Therefore, as I said unto mine apostles I say unto you again, that every soul who believeth on your words, and is baptized by water for the remission of sins, shall receive the Holy Ghost (D&C 84:64).

Visual Aid:
GAPK 602
The Gift of the Holy Ghost

4. I partake of the sacrament to renew my baptismal covenant with Heavenly Father.

Your baptism day is a wonderful day. You feel clean and pure. You may strongly feel the Spirit of the Lord. You probably feel a deep desire to keep those good feelings.

Unfortunately, it's easy to forget. It's also easy to commit sins. Even small sins can keep you from feeling the Spirit. They can keep you from returning to Heavenly Father.

This is why Heavenly Father gave us the sacrament. He knows that we often forget important things. He also knows that we can't stay perfectly clean after baptism. The sacrament helps us remember the Savior Jesus Christ. And it makes us clean again when we repent. The sacrament is a wonderful gift from Heavenly Father.

Thought Question: How do you feel when you take the sacrament and think about the Savior?

Scripture
And this shall ye do in remembrance of my body, which I have shown unto you. And it shall be a testimony unto the Father that ye do always remember me. And if ye do always remember me ye shall have my Spirit to be with you (3 Nephi 18:7).

Visual Aid:
GAPK 604
Passing the Sacrament

Chapter 7

July: My family can follow Jesus Christ in faith

Happiness in family life is most likely to be achieved when founded upon the teachings of the Lord Jesus Christ.

—"The Family: A Proclamation to the World"

Scripture

And Adam and Eve blessed the name of God, and they made all things known unto their sons and their daughters (Moses 5:12).

Visual Aid:
GAPK 119
Adam and Eve Teaching Their Children

1. I can learn about righteous families by reading the scriptures.

Adam and Eve were the first man and woman. They were also the first family. We can learn about righteous family life by studying their family. The scriptures teach that Adam and Eve worked together. They had sons and daughters. They obeyed God's commandments.

Angels taught Adam about the Savior and the plan of salvation. Adam and Eve were "glad" and "blessed the name of God" when they learned that they could be saved (Moses 5:11–12). They taught all these things to their family. They also wrote them in a book.

We can help our family become like Adam and Eve's family. We can work together and obey the commandments. We can learn the gospel together. We can rejoice because we know the plan of salvation.

Thought Question: Which righteous family do you like to read about in the scriptures?

2. I can learn about my family history.

When even one person joins the Church, he can change history. The first person in a family to follow Jesus Christ by being baptized is a pioneer. If you or your parents are the first members of the Church in your family, that means that you are pioneers!

Do you know very much about your family pioneers? Do you know who joined the Church first in your family? Where did they live? What language did they speak? What sacrifices or changes did they have to make? Do you know any stories about them? All of these things are part of your family history.

Stories about our family pioneers can help strengthen our faith in Jesus Christ.

Thought Question: Can you share a story about the first member of your family to join the Church?

Scripture
And this shall be our covenant—that we will walk in all the ordinances of the Lord (D&C 136:4).

Visual Aid:
GAPK 601
Baptism

3. I will honor my father and mother and show respect for others in my family.

Scripture

Honour thy father and thy mother: that thy days may be long upon the land which the Lord thy God giveth thee (Exodus 20:12).

When Elder Neal A. Maxwell was a boy, he worked hard for his family. He raised pigs and helped on the farm. He said sometimes he didn't try very hard to do a good job. One day his father asked him to pound some fence posts into the ground. Neal decided to do his very best. He "worked hard all day." Then he waited for his father to come home. His father looked carefully at the fence posts. He even measured to make sure they were straight. Then he praised Neal's good job. Neal felt happy that he had tried to do his best for his father.[8]

When we honor our parents in righteousness, we feel good, and so do they. They will teach us how to become good, strong people. They will also help lead us home to Heavenly Father.

Thought Question: What can you do to show respect for your family members?

Visual Aid:
GAPK 606
Family Prayer

4. My family can follow Jesus Christ in faith by holding family home evening.

When President Gordon B. Hinckley was a boy, President Joseph F. Smith asked the members of the Church to have family home evening. Gordon's father said that their family would do it. They warmed up the parlor, sang songs, played games, and told stories. The children took turns giving "performances" for each other. Sometimes they giggled and teased each other, but their parents persisted.

President Hinckley said that "those simple little meetings" strengthened their family. They felt more love for each other. They felt God's love more strongly in their home. President Hinckley promised that our families can grow in faith through family home evening.[9]

Thought Question: How has your family been blessed by praying or learning the gospel together?

Scripture
And all thy children shall be taught of the Lord; and great shall be the peace of thy children (Isaiah 54:13).

Visual Aid:
GAPK 616
Family Togetherness

Chapter 8

August: My faith in Jesus Christ grows when I listen to the Holy Ghost

For behold, the Comforter knoweth all things, and beareth record of the Father and of the Son.

—D&C 42:17

1. A testimony is a spiritual witness given by the Holy Ghost.

Scripture
And by the power of the Holy Ghost ye may know the truth of all things (Moroni 10:5).

Heavenly Father sends the Holy Ghost to teach us that His Church is true. When you know in your heart that the gospel is true, you have a testimony.

The five fingers of your hand can help you remember the most important parts of a testimony:

1. Heavenly Father lives.
2. His son, Jesus Christ, is the Savior of the world.
3. Joseph Smith is a prophet of God; he translated the Book of Mormon by the power of God.
4. The Church of Jesus Christ of Latter-day Saints is God's true Church.
5. We have a living prophet.

Heavenly Father promises that His Spirit will teach you "the truth of all things" (Moroni 10:5).

Thought Question: Can you bear your testimony of an important part of the gospel?

Visual Aid:
Use the fingers on your hand to count off the important parts of your testimony.

2. I can invite the promptings of the Holy Ghost.

God commanded the prophet Lehi to take his family into the wilderness. He also sent them a special compass called the Liahona. Like any compass, the Liahona showed them which direction to travel. But it didn't just point north like an ordinary compass. It pointed the way that Heavenly Father wanted them to go. Sometimes writing also appeared on it.

When Lehi and his family lived righteously, the compass worked for them. But when they disobeyed, it stopped working. They did not know which way to go.

The Holy Ghost is like the Liahona for us. When we live worthily, we help the Holy Ghost to speak to us (Alma 37:38–45). Guidance from the Holy Ghost is a special gift from Heavenly Father. It can help us return home to Him.

Thought Question: How has praying, studying the scriptures, keeping the commandments, or following the living prophets helped you feel the Spirit?

Scripture
For behold, it is as easy to give heed to the word of Christ, which will point to you a straight course to eternal bliss, as it was for our fathers to give heed to this compass, which would point unto them a straight course to the promised land (Alma 37:44).

Visual Aid:
GAPK 302
The Liahona

3. I can recognize the promptings of the Holy Ghost.

Scripture

And after the earthquake a fire; but the Lord was not in the fire: and after the fire a still small voice (1 Kings 19:12).

Visual Aid:
GAPK 617
Search the Scriptures

The prophet Elijah once needed some direction from the Lord. He stood in a cave on a mountain and waited for the Lord to speak to him.

First a "great and strong wind" came by and broke the rocks in pieces. "But the Lord was not in the wind." Next there was an earthquake. "But the Lord was not in the earthquake." After the earthquake came a fire. "But the Lord was not in the fire." At last there was a "still small voice." That was the Lord's voice (1 Kings 19:11–12).

When we feel the Holy Ghost in our hearts, we usually feel quiet, peaceful, and good. It is a hard feeling to describe, but it gets easier to recognize the more we feel it. We should live to be worthy of the Holy Ghost's help. We should pray and ask for it. Then we should be careful to listen for the answers.

Thought Question: What are some ways that the Spirit has spoken to you?

4. The Holy Ghost testifies of Jesus Christ and can teach, guide, warn, protect, and comfort me.

President Thomas S. Monson once visited a tiny village in Samoa. He spoke to a group of almost two hundred children. As the meeting ended, President Monson had a strong feeling that he should greet each child, one by one. He looked at his watch. He didn't have very much time. But the Spirit whispered strongly that he needed to shake each child's hand. So he decided to stay a while longer.

When he told the children's teacher his decision, the teacher smiled. He said that the children had wanted to meet an apostle of God. They had prayed that President Monson would stay to shake their hands. Everyone knew that the Spirit had answered their prayers by telling President Monson to stay.[10]

Thought Question: How has the Spirit helped you?

Scripture
Yea, behold, I will tell you in your mind and in your heart, by the Holy Ghost, which shall come upon you and which shall dwell in your heart (D&C 8:2).

Visual Aid:
GAPK 605
Young Boy Praying

Chapter 9

September: My faith in Jesus Christ grows when I serve others

When ye are in the service of your fellow beings
ye are only in the service of your God.

—Mosiah 2:17

1. Jesus Christ taught us to serve others.

Scripture
For I have given you an example, that ye should do as I have done to you (John 13:15).

Before the Atonement, Jesus and His apostles had the Last Supper together. He taught them and performed the first sacrament. Then He took a towel, poured water in a bowl, and started to wash the apostles' feet. Peter did not want the Lord to wash his feet. He did not think that Jesus should act like a servant because Jesus was the king. But Jesus taught him that the Lord serves His children, and we should serve each other. Then Peter let Jesus wash his feet.

Jesus said, "I have given you an example, that ye should do as I have done to you" (John 13:15). We should try to be like Jesus. We should serve each other because He serves us each day.

Thought Questions: How has someone served you? How have you served others?

Visual Aid:
GAPK 226
Jesus Washing the Apostles' Feet

2. I will serve in my family.

When the prophet Lehi and his family were in the wilderness, they had to hunt animals for food. One day Nephi's bow broke. He could not shoot animals. The whole family was hungry. Some of them were angry, and even Lehi complained.

Nephi remembered the Lord. He did not complain. He made a bow and arrows out of wood. Then he asked his father, the prophet, where he should go to find food. Lehi repented. He asked the Lord where to go, and the Lord told him. Nephi obeyed the Lord and his father. He brought back food for his family.

Nephi served his family by getting food for them. He also served them by setting a good example for them, even when they were complaining (1 Nephi 16:17–32).

Thought Question: How can you serve your family?

Scripture
And it came to pass that I, Nephi, did make out of wood a bow, and out of a straight stick, an arrow; wherefore, I did arm myself with a bow and an arrow, with a sling and with stones. And I said unto my father: Whither shall I go to obtain food? (1 Nephi 16:23)

Visual Aid:
GAPK 301
Lehi's Family Leaving Jerusalem

Scripture

For, brethren, ye have been called unto liberty; only use not liberty for an occasion to the flesh, but by love serve one another (Galatians 5:13).

Visual Aid:
GAPK 615
Serving One Another

3. I will serve others by treating them kindly and sharing what I have.

When President Thomas S. Monson was a boy, he got an electric train for Christmas. His mother also bought a little windup train for a neighbor boy named Mark, whose family was poor. Tommy saw that the windup train had a tanker car that his train didn't have. He talked his mother into giving it to him instead of giving it to Mark.

On Christmas day, they took the windup train to Mark's house. Tommy saw how happy Mark was. He felt bad for keeping the tanker car. He said, "We forgot to bring two cars that should go with your train!" Then he ran home and got the tanker car and another one of his own cars for Mark. President Monson says he "felt a joy difficult to describe and impossible to forget."[11]

Thought Questions: How have you been blessed by someone else's kindness? How have you blessed someone else?

4. As I serve others, I serve Jesus Christ and show my love for Him.

The Church hymnbook has a song called "A Poor Wayfaring Man of Grief." The song tells the story of a person who meets a stranger and helps him. The person in the song gives the man food and water, rescues him from prison, and helps him in other ways. At the end of the song, the stranger removes his "disguise." The person in the song is surprised to see that the stranger is the Savior (*Hymns*, no. 29).

Jesus taught that anything we do for God's children, we also do for Him. When serving others is hard, we can remember that all of us are children of God. We can remember that we are also serving Jesus Christ.

Thought Question: Why are you serving the Savior when you serve other people?

Scripture
And the King shall answer and say unto them, Verily I say unto you, Inasmuch as ye have done it unto one of the least of these my brethren, ye have done it unto me (Matthew 25:40).

Visual Aid:
GAPK 239
The Resurrected Christ

Chapter 10

October: I show my faith in Jesus Christ when I share the gospel with others

*Let your light so shine before men,
that they may see your good works, and
glorify your Father which is in heaven.*

—Matthew 5:16

Scripture

Ye are the light of the world. A city that is set on an hill cannot be hid. Neither do men light a candle, and put it under a bushel, but on a candlestick; and it giveth light unto all that are in the house (Matthew 5:14–15).

Visual Aid:
GAPK 520
Gordon B. Hinckley

1. I will be a good example to others by the way I live.

President Gordon B. Hinckley told about a young man who, as a boy, had lived near many Church members. They made fun of him and called him names. No one made friends with him. He decided that he hated Mormons.

When he was in high school, his family moved. In his new town, he made a good friend for the first time in his life. One day, he saw his friend reading a book. He asked what the book was. The friend replied, "The Book of Mormon. Would you like to read it?" He replied, "No!" Over a long time, the friend patiently taught him about the Church and took him to Church activities. At last he decided to read the Book of Mormon. The Holy Ghost blessed him with a testimony, and he was baptized.

President Hinckley said, "This kind of miracle . . . will happen when there is kindness, respect, and love."[12]

Thought Question: How have other people's examples affected you?

2. My testimony grows when I share it and hear the testimonies of others.

A testimony is like your muscles. If you exercise and use your muscles every day, they will grow stronger. If you look for chances to share your testimony, it will grow stronger every time you bear it.

Elder Steven E. Snow said that he bore his testimony for the first time on the day he was confirmed. He said, "As I spoke, a wonderful, warm feeling filled my heart." The Spirit taught him that "joining the church was the right thing to do." He gained a testimony by bearing his testimony.[13] We can bear our testimonies in church meetings, during family home evening, and when we're with our friends. A testimony can be short and simple, but sharing blesses us and others.

Thought Question: How has sharing your testimony strengthened it?

Scripture
For we cannot but speak the things which we have seen and heard (Acts 4:20).

Visual Aid:
GAPK 607
Young Girl Speaking at Church

3. I will invite my friends to Primary.

Scripture
For there is no respect of persons with God (Romans 2:11).

Many of us started Primary when we were three. Before that we went to nursery. For as long as we can remember, we've been coming to church! Now imagine if you were coming to Primary for the first time. What if you didn't know any of the teachers or children? What if you didn't know which class to sit with? What if everyone was using words you'd never heard before, like "resurrection" or "agency"?

You might feel confused, scared, or shy. You would like it if the teachers and children smiled at you and welcomed you. You would be glad if they explained new words or told you what would happen next. You would like to have a friend to sit with. If people treated you kindly, you would probably want to return the next week!

Thought Question: What could you say to a new friend at Primary?

Visual Aid:
no picture

4. I will prepare now to become a missionary.

To be a missionary, a person has to prepare. Missionaries get up early in the morning. Do you go to bed on time and get up early? You are preparing to be a missionary! Missionaries have to work hard all day. Do you eat good food, get exercise, and work hard? You are preparing to be a missionary! Missionaries have to take care of themselves. Are you learning to do laundry, cook, and plan your day? You are preparing to be a missionary!

Most of all, missionaries teach the gospel. Do you study the scriptures, pray, share your testimony, and keep the commandments? You are preparing to be a missionary!

Thought Question: How are you preparing to be a missionary?

Scripture
Let no man despise thy youth; but be thou an example of the believers, in word, in conversation, in charity, in spirit, in faith, in purity
(1 Timothy 4:12).

Visual Aid:
GAPK 612
Missionaries Teach the Gospel of Jesus Christ

Chapter 11

November: My faith in Jesus Christ blesses my life. I am thankful for my blessings

Thou shalt thank the Lord thy God in all things.

—D&C 59:7

1. I am thankful for my home and family.

Scripture

Children, obey your parents in all things: for this is well pleasing unto the Lord (Colossians 3:20).

Mary Fielding Smith was the mother of President Joseph Fielding Smith. When Joseph Fielding was a boy, Mary's husband, Hyrum, was killed with the Prophet Joseph Smith. Mary went west with the Saints. She had to take her small children and travel on her own. The captain of the wagon company did not think she could make it. He said she would slow the wagon train down. But Mary told him that she would make it by herself, and she would beat him to the valley.

Through prayer and faith in the Lord, Mary and her family made it to the Salt Lake Valley—and they beat the captain there!

President Joseph Fielding Smith learned from his mother's faith and independence, and he expressed deep gratitude for them.[14]

Thought Question: What are some of the blessings that come from your home and family?

Visual Aid:
GAPK 412
Mary Fielding and Joseph F. Smith Crossing the Plains

2. I am thankful for my membership in the Church of Jesus Christ.

President Joseph Fielding Smith was a boy when he and his mother Mary came to the Salt Lake Valley as pioneers. They were very poor, but when summer came, they had a crop of potatoes. Mary took the best potatoes to the tithing office. The clerk thought that Mary shouldn't have to pay tithing because she was so poor. Mary told him, "You ought to be ashamed of yourself. Would you deny me a blessing? If I did not pay my tithing I should expect the Lord to withhold His blessings from me; I pay my tithing, not only because it is a law of God, but because I expect a blessing by doing it."[15]

Sometimes we have to make sacrifices to keep the commandments. If we are humble, we can always see how the sacrifices bring blessings.

Thought Question: How have you been blessed through your membership in the Church?

Scripture
And that the gathering together upon the land of Zion, and upon her stakes, may be for a defense, and for a refuge from the storm, and from wrath when it shall be poured out without mixture upon the whole earth (D&C 115:6).

Visual Aid:
GAPK 412
Mary Fielding and Joseph F. Smith Crossing the Plains

Scripture

And they cast out many devils, and anointed with oil many that were sick, and healed them (Mark 6:13).

Visual Aid:
GAPK 613
Administering to the Sick

3. I am thankful for the priesthood, and I am blessed by it.

Elder Gene R. Cook grew up in a less-active family. Then Gene's big brother, Ron, started going to church and taking Gene with him. One day Ron got a terrible pain in his stomach. Their mother called an ambulance. Ron asked his father for a priesthood blessing. The boys weren't sure their dad knew how to give a blessing, but he laid his hands on Ron's head and blessed him. Ron jumped up. He had no more pain.

Later, the doctor said it sounded like Ron's appendix had ruptured. Ron told Gene, "When Dad put his hands on my head, I felt the Spirit of the Lord go through my whole body. I know the priesthood is real." Ron's faith helped the family return to the Church. They were blessed by the priesthood.[16]

Thought Question: How have you been blessed by the priesthood?

4. I will show my gratitude and love for Heavenly Father and Jesus Christ by keeping Their commandments.

President Thomas S. Monson served in the United States Navy in World War II. There were 250 young men in his company. Every night, one soldier would kneel by his bunk and pray. The other men laughed at him and made fun of him for praying. But President Monson said, "He never wavered. He never faltered. He had courage."

Heavenly Father and Jesus Christ have given us many wonderful blessings. They only ask that we keep the commandments. It may take courage, but President Monson says we should "muster courage for the conflicts, courage to say no, courage to say yes, for courage counts."[17]

Thought Question: Can you think about a time when you had to find courage to keep the commandments?

Scripture
For God hath not given us the spirit of fear; but of power, and of love, and of a sound mind (2 Timothy 1:7).

Visual Aid:
GAPK 605
Young Boy Praying

Chapter 12

December: Jesus Christ once lived on the earth, and I have faith that He will come again

This same Jesus, which is taken up from you into heaven, shall so come in like manner as ye have seen him go into heaven.

—Acts 1:11

1. Ancient prophets foretold the coming of the Savior to the earth.

Scripture
Yea, and all the prophets from Samuel and those that follow after, as many as have spoken, have likewise foretold of these days (Acts 3:24).

Nephi's father, the prophet Lehi, had a vision of a tree. The tree had wonderful white fruit. Nephi prayed that he could see the vision and know what it meant. An angel appeared and showed Nephi the vision. Nephi saw Mary, the mother of Jesus. He saw Jesus as a baby. He saw John the Baptist baptize the Savior. He saw Jesus teaching and preaching, and he saw the people crucify Him.

Then the angel asked Nephi if he knew what the tree meant. Nephi said it was the love of God. Heavenly Father wants all His children to know of His love. Since the world began, He has sent prophets to teach us about the Savior and the plan of salvation.

Thought Question: Why was it important for people to know that the Savior would come someday?

Visual Aid:
GAPK 113
Isaiah Writes of Christ's Birth

2. The Savior Jesus Christ came to earth as a baby born in Bethlehem.

For thousands of years, the people of Israel waited for their Savior to come. At last Jesus Christ was born in a small town called Bethlehem. That night, shepherds were out in the fields, watching over their sheep. Suddenly an angel appeared to them in a bright light. The shepherds were frightened, but the angel told them not to be afraid. The angel told them that the Savior was born and that they should go to the city and find him. Then the shepherds could see thousands of angels, all singing for joy! The shepherds hurried to Bethlehem. They found a little stable. They saw Mary and Joseph and the baby Jesus. They knew that the Savior had come to earth at last. They ran to tell everyone!

Thought Question: Imagine that you were one of the shepherds who saw the angel. How would you feel?

Scripture
And the angel said unto them, Fear not: for, behold, I bring you good tidings of great joy, which shall be to all people.
For unto you is born this day in the city of David a Saviour, which is Christ the Lord (Luke 2:10–11).

Visual Aid:
GAPK 202
The Announcement of Christ's Birth to the Shepherds

Scripture

And he spake unto the multitude, and said unto them: Behold your little ones. And as they looked to behold they cast their eyes towards heaven, and they saw the heavens open, and they saw angels descending out of heaven as it were in the midst of fire; and they came down and encircled those little ones about, and they were encircled about with fire; and the angels did minister unto them (3 Nephi 17:23–24).

Visual Aid:
GAPK 322
Jesus Blesses the Nephite Children

3. I can have peace, happiness, and love because of the coming of Jesus Christ.

When Jesus visited the people in America, He taught them the gospel. He healed everyone who was sick or hurt. Then He asked them to bring their little children to Him. Jesus prayed for the people and wept. Then "he took their little children, one by one, and blessed them, and prayed unto the Father for them." He told the people, "Behold your little ones" (3 Nephi 17:21–23).

When the people looked up, they saw angels come down from heaven. The angels surrounded the little children and blessed them.

Jesus loves children today as much as he loved the children in America then. When He comes again, he will probably call for the children, bless them, and love them. We can look forward to that wonderful day.

Thought Question: How will you feel when someday you meet the Savior again?

4. As I follow Jesus Christ in faith, I prepare myself for the Second Coming.

Someday Jesus Christ will return to the earth. When that wonderful time comes, there will be no more wars or hunger. People will live in love and peace. Everyone will be working hard to share the gospel. They will also find the names of people who have died and do the temple work for them. Everyone will be busy and happy.

We can live now to be ready for that time. We can try hard to be kind and happy. We can make our homes peaceful and safe. We can share the gospel with our friends. We can do our family history work. Then, when the Savior comes again, we will be ready to do His work with Him.

Thought Question: How can we prepare for the Savior's second coming?

Scripture
Prepare ye, prepare ye for that which is to come, for the Lord is nigh (D&C 1:12).

Visual Aid:
GAPK 238
The Second Coming

References

1. Sheri Dew, *Ezra Taft Benson: A Biography* (Salt Lake City: Deseret Book, 1987), 32–39.

1. Spencer W. Kimball, *Faith Precedes the Miracle* (Salt Lake City: Deseret Book, 1972), 256.

2. Jeffrey R. Holland, "Broken Things to Mend," *Ensign*, May 2006, 69.

3. *Teachings of Presidents of the Church: Heber J. Grant* (Salt Lake City: The Church of Jesus Christ of Latter-day Saints, 2002), 43.

4. *Teachings of Presidents of the Church: Wilford Woodruff* (Salt Lake City: The Church of Jesus Christ of Latter-day Saints, 2004), xix–xx.

5. Brent L. Top, "'I Was with My Family': Joseph Smith—Devoted Husband, Father, Son, and Brother," *Ensign*, August 1991, 22.

6. Patricia Reece Roper, "We Have to Try!" *Friend*, March 2004, 9.

7. Richard G. Hinckley, "Repentance, a Blessing of Membership," *Ensign*, May 2006, 48.

8. Neal A. Maxwell, "Put Your Shoulder to the Wheel," *Ensign*, May 1998, 37.

9. Gordon B. Hinckley, "Family Home Evening," *Ensign*, March 2003, 3.

10. Thomas S. Monson, "Frame Your Life with Faith," *Friend*, July 2006, 2.

11. Thomas S. Monson, "Mark's Train," *Friend*, October 1977, 16.

12. Gordon B. Hinckley, "The Need for Greater Kindness," *Ensign*, May 2006, 58–61.

13. Hilary M. Hendricks and Steven E. Snow, "Friend to Friend: The Beginning of a Testimony," *Friend*, March 2004, 6.

14. Jane McBride Choate, "Mary Fielding Smith—Mother in Israel," *Friend*, July 1993, 32.

15. Ibid.

16. Barbara Jean Jones and Gene R. Cook, "Friend to Friend: A Brother's Example," *Friend*, December 2005, 8.

17. Thomas S. Monson, "Courage Counts," *Friend*, November 2005, 2.

About the Author

Lee Ann Setzer was born in the Mojave Desert in Southern California. She has lived in Utah for more than twenty years. She served in the Japan Sendai Mission and still likes raw fish. She graduated from Brigham Young University with a bachelor's and then a master's degree in speech-language pathology.

Lee Ann is the author of several books, including *I Am Ready for Baptism,* the *Sariah McDuff* series, *Tiny Talks Volume 6,* and *Gathered: a Novel of Ruth.*

Lee Ann and her husband have three children, who all like to talk and write. They live in Utah.

About the Illustrator

Whether producing DVDs for top corporations or illustrating children's books, Glenn Harmon is driven by a love for creating. While Glenn is gifted in traditional forms of illustration, he enjoys the challenge of creating digital art. He is currently completing a degree in animation and production at Brigham Young University. Glenn resides in Provo, Utah, with his wife, Kristen, and son, Maxwell. His books include, *The Wisemen of Bountiful* and *I Am Ready for Baptism!*